Cambridge Plays

Coyote Girl

Rosalind Kerven

Illustrated by Amanda Hall

Characters

Narrator *the person who tells the story*

Grandmother Spider *a very kind, magical old woman*

Yellow Corn Maiden *a cross, spiteful girl*

Blue Corn Maiden *a gentle, sweet girl*

First Hunter *a quiet, gloomy man*

Second Hunter *a cheerful, friendly man*

CAMBRIDGE
UNIVERSITY PRESS

Scene 1

One afternoon in a Hopi village

Narrator	There were two girls who said they were best friends. But one day they had a big argument.
Blue Corn Maiden	I don't like this game, Yellow Corn Maiden. It's boring!
Yellow Corn Maiden	You spoil everything, Blue Corn Maiden. I won't be your friend if you don't play it.
Blue Corn Maiden	In that case, I'm going home!
Narrator	Blue Corn Maiden ran off crying.
Yellow Corn Maiden	Huh! I'll make that stupid Blue Corn Maiden sorry! I'll play a trick on her, that's what I'll do – a really horrid trick, one that works by *magic*!

Scene 2

The next morning

Narrator	The next morning, Yellow Corn Maiden went round to Blue Corn Maiden's house and pretended to be sorry.
Yellow Corn Maiden	Hey, Blue Corn Maiden, let's be friends again. Come outside and play.
Blue Corn Maiden	I don't feel like playing.
Yellow Corn Maiden	Don't be silly. Let's go up the hill and I'll show you a secret.
Blue Corn Maiden	What secret?
Yellow Corn Maiden	I'm not telling. You'll have to wait and see!
Narrator	Yellow Corn Maiden led the way to a quiet spot outside the village. There she pulled something strange and beautiful out of her dress.

Yellow Corn Maiden	Look, this is my secret. I don't want anyone except you to see it, Blue Corn Maiden.
Blue Corn Maiden	What beautiful, sparkly colours! But what is it?
Yellow Corn Maiden	It's a rainbow wheel. Look, I'll throw it up in the air. Now – quickly, Blue Corn Maiden – catch it!

Narrator Blue Corn Maiden woke up and whimpered like a dog.

Second Hunter No – stop – don't shoot it! There's something odd about that animal.

First Hunter You're right. It seems very tame.

Second Hunter Here, coyote, come here. We won't hurt you.

Narrator He held out his hand. The coyote girl crept forward and rubbed her grey head against his fingers.

First Hunter It *is* behaving very oddly. What shall we do with it?

Second Hunter I know! We ought to take it to the old magic woman, Grandmother Spider.

Scene 4

The next day, in the desert

Narrator The hunters tied up the coyote girl's paws so that she could not escape. Then they set off on their journey, taking turns to carry her on their backs.

First Hunter	Phew! It's so hot in this desert. We seem to have been walking all day. I'm worn out.
Second Hunter	I know. But look, the sun's setting – and there's Grandmother Spider's house!
First Hunter	It's a very strange place.
Second Hunter	That's just the door we can see. The house itself is under the ground.

__Second Hunter__ knocks at the door.

First and Second Hunters together	Grandmother Spider! Look – we've brought you a present.
Narrator	A dark shape climbed out of the underground house.
First Hunter	What a strange thing!
Second Hunter	It looks like an enormous grey spider.
First Hunter	No – I think it's a person, wrapped in a big grey cloak.
Second Hunter	You're right. It's an old woman . . . it's Spider Woman!
Narrator	Spider Woman's hair was silver. Her face was a maze of wrinkles. Her dress was a shimmer of cobwebs.
First and Second Hunters together	Grandmother Spider, please help us!

Grandmother Spider	Welcome, my grandchildren. Of course I'll help you. What have you brought me?
Second Hunter	It's a coyote, Grandmother Spider – but there's something very odd about it.
Grandmother Spider	Let me have a look at it.
Narrator	Blue Corn Maiden began to whimper.
Grandmother Spider	You're quite right. This is not an ordinary coyote. Oh, the poor thing! Someone has put a nasty magic spell on it.
Narrator	Blue Corn Maiden howled loudly.
Second Hunter	A magic spell? How terrible! Can you do anything to help?
Grandmother Spider	Of course I can. Don't worry, little one, I'll soon set you free.

Scene 5

Inside Grandmother Spider's house

Grandmother Spider Now, little coyote, you wait here with me. I've sent the men to fetch the things I need to take that nasty spell off you.

*The door opens. The **Hunters** come in.*

First and Second Hunters together	Grandmother Spider, we're back. We've got lots of leaves and berries.
Grandmother Spider	Good. Now, watch.
Narrator	Grandmother Spider dropped the leaves and berries into a huge pot and filled it up with water. Then she hung the pot over her fire.

Grandmother Spider	There, the water's nice and warm now. Come on, little coyote, jump in!
Narrator	The coyote girl knew Spider Woman was kind and wanted to help her. So she jumped into the pot with a loud SPLASH!
First Hunter	What a lot of steam! I can't see a thing.
Grandmother Spider	Don't worry.
Narrator	Grandmother Spider twisted and turned the coyote girl about in the water. The coyote girl felt warm and safe there. She whimpered happily, as Spider Woman sang a sweet magic song.
Grandmother Spider	There, I've finished. Now, I'll pull the coyote out and wrap it in a great big blanket.

Narrator
Carefully, Spider Woman took the blanket away.

First Hunter
Well, well, well! What a surprise! It's a *girl*!

Grandmother Spider
You poor thing! What's your name, little one?

Blue Corn Maiden
Oh please, I'm Blue Corn Maiden.

Grandmother Spider
And who put that nasty spell on you?

Blue Corn Maiden
It was Yellow Corn Maiden.

Grandmother Spider
Well, she has been a very wicked girl. But don't worry, it is all over now. And soon I shall punish her. But first I will send you safely home to your mother and father.

Scene 6

Back in the village

Narrator	When Blue Corn Maiden got home to her own village, her mother and father rushed up to hug and kiss her.
Blue Corn Maiden	I'm so happy to be home again!
Narrator	The next day, Yellow Corn Maiden came round to see her.
Yellow Corn Maiden	Hi, Blue Corn Maiden, it's me. I've come to say sorry.
Blue Corn Maiden	Oh well, I suppose I have to forgive you.
Yellow Corn Maiden	That's great. (Ha, ha, I'm not really sorry!) Come on, Blue Corn Maiden, let's go up to the spring and fetch some water together.
Blue Corn Maiden	All right then.

Narrator	When they reached the spring, Blue Corn Maiden took out a cup and filled it with water.
Yellow Corn Maiden	Hey, that's a beautiful cup you've got there. Let me drink from it.
Blue Corn Maiden	No, don't touch it! Grandmother Spider gave it to me.
Yellow Corn Maiden	Who's she? What are you talking about? Give it to me!
Narrator	Yellow Corn Maiden snatched the cup rudely, and drank from it. There was a sudden flash, and Yellow Corn Maiden made a strange noise.
Yellow Corn Maiden	Ssssss!
	***Blue Corn Maiden** screams.*
Blue Corn Maiden	Oh my goodness! Yellow Corn Maiden's turned into a snake!

__Grandmother Spider__ suddenly appears.

Grandmother Spider

Yes indeed, when Yellow Corn Maiden drank from my magic cup, it turned her into a snake. *That* was her punishment and that was the end of her.

So remember this story, children, and remember what I have taught you. Do not hurt your friends. Instead, try to be kind to everyone, and live together in peace.

About the people who told this story

This story comes from the Hopi Indians, who live in the south-west of the United States. The Hopi are unusual because even today many of them are able to live in their own special way.

The Hopi live in thirteen villages built high up in the dry lands of Arizona. Although there is little rain and few plants grow there, they are skilled corn farmers. Their houses are made of sun-dried bricks or *adobe*. Traditionally the women make pottery and baskets, while the men weave cloth and hunt. They are known as the 'peaceful people' and they have always worked hard to live in peace.